Learn the ABCs
Dd
Warren Rylands and
Jared Siemens
LIGHTBOX
openlightbox.com

Go to **www.openlightbox.com** and enter this book's unique code.

ACCESS CODE

LBXA5744

Lightbox is an all-inclusive digital solution for the teaching and learning of curriculum topics in an original, groundbreaking way. Lightbox is based on National Curriculum Standards.

OPTIMIZED FOR

- ✓ TABLETS
- ✓ WHITEBOARDS
- ✓ COMPUTERS
- ✓ AND MUCH MORE!

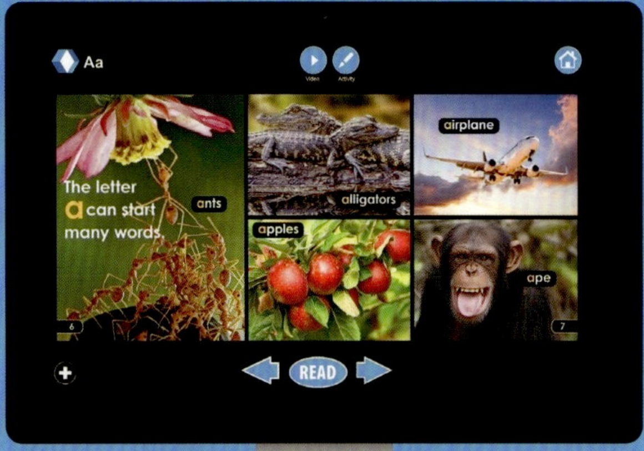

STANDARD FEATURES OF LIGHTBOX

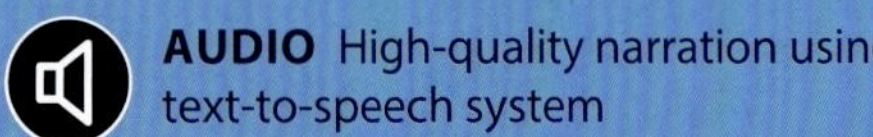
AUDIO High-quality narration using text-to-speech system

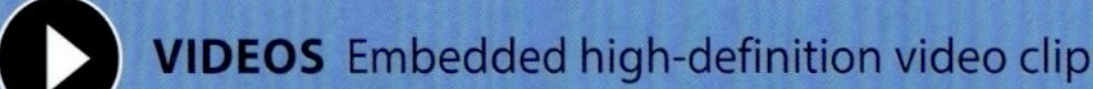
VIDEOS Embedded high-definition video clips

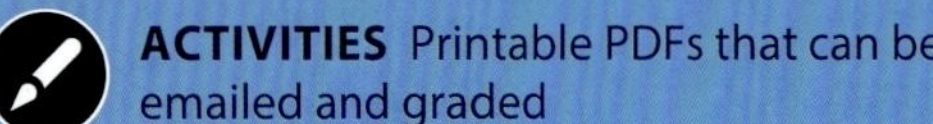
ACTIVITIES Printable PDFs that can be emailed and graded

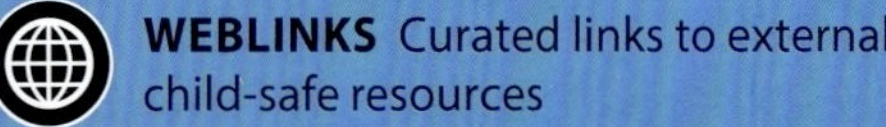
WEBLINKS Curated links to external, child-safe resources

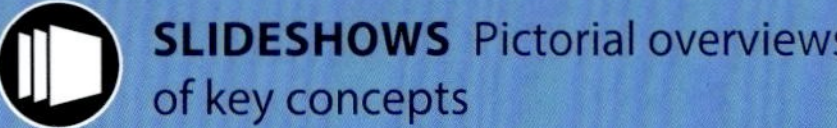
SLIDESHOWS Pictorial overviews of key concepts

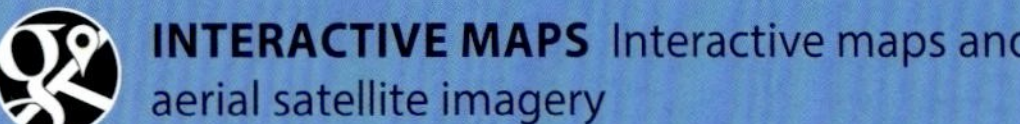
INTERACTIVE MAPS Interactive maps and aerial satellite imagery

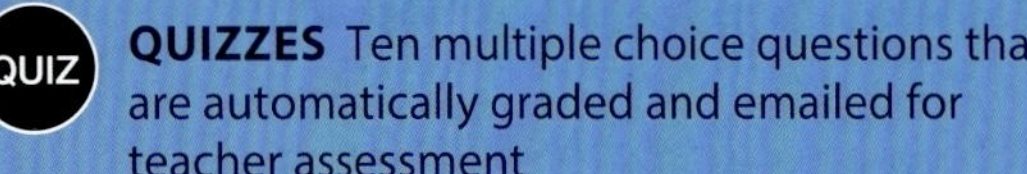
QUIZZES Ten multiple choice questions that are automatically graded and emailed for teacher assessment

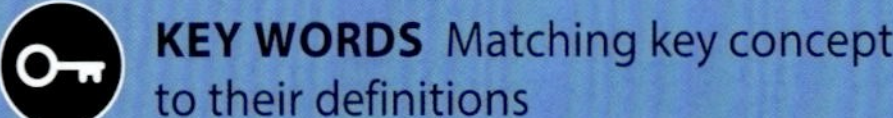
KEY WORDS Matching key concepts to their definitions

VIDEOS

WEBLINKS

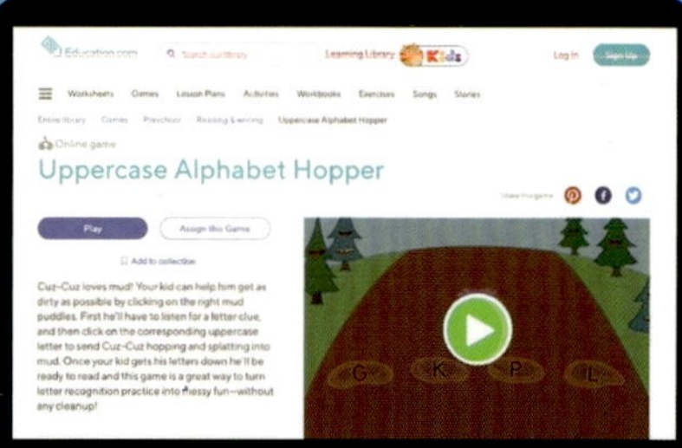

SLIDESHOWS

QUIZZES

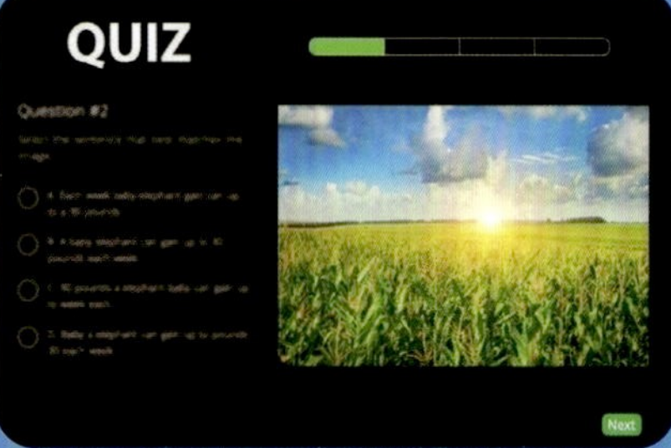

This title is part of our Lightbox digital subscription

1-Year K–5 Subscription
ISBN 978-1-5105-5712-3

Access hundreds of Lightbox titles with our digital subscription.
Sign up for a **FREE** subscription trial at **www.openlightbox.com/trial**

Dd

CONTENTS

Let's discover the letter

This is an uppercase D

This is how you write it

This is a lowercase d

This is how you write it

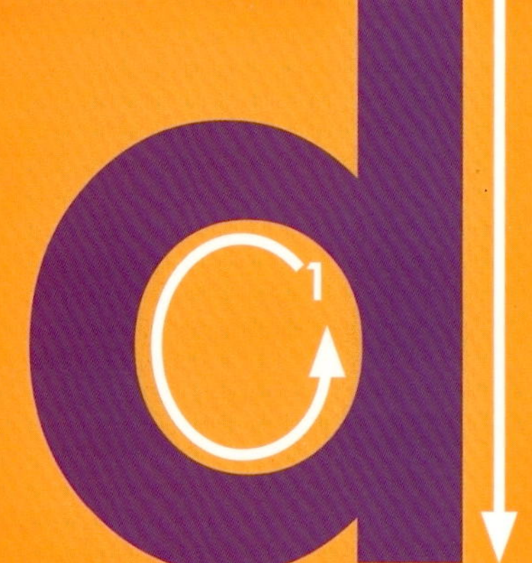

The letter
d can start
many words.
dinosaur
dime
OF AMERICA
E PLURIBUS UNUM
DIME
DOLLAR

duck
dolphin
dog
STATES OF AMERICA
E·PLURIBUS·UNUM
ONE DIME
QUART

The letter d
can be inside
a word.

URITY
CEMENT
JUSTICE FOR ALL
ICER
badge
lemonade
spider
goldfish

The letter d can be at the end of a word.

bread

Many names start with an uppercase D.

Donna drinks water.

Deb loves presents.

David likes hot chocolate.

Dorothy is tall.

Darwin makes good pizza.

The letter d makes different sounds.

bridge

doll

The letter d makes a d sound in the word doll.

The letter d makes a j sound in the word bridge.

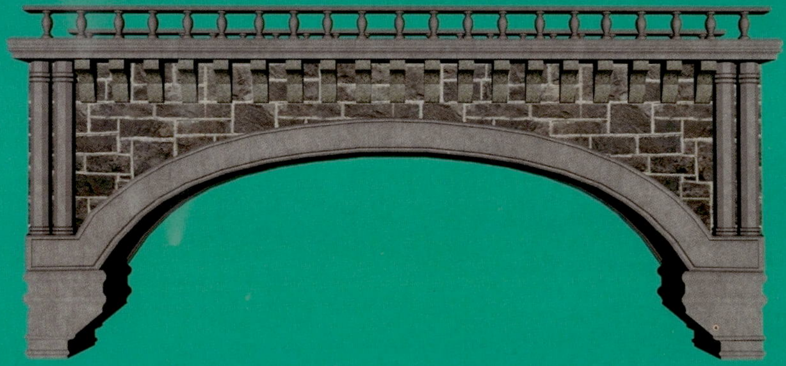

The letter d makes a d sound in most words

food

day

need

Sometimes the letter d makes a j sound.

wedge

judge

edge

Having Fun with D

Doug the dog loved to dig.

He often dug dozens of holes in the dirt.

One day, Doug called his best friend Dan the duck. He asked Dan to help him dig.

Doug wanted to dig the deepest hole ever dug.

Dan lived on a pond near Denali. Doug lived in a big yard in Delaware.

Dan the duck reached Delaware many days later.

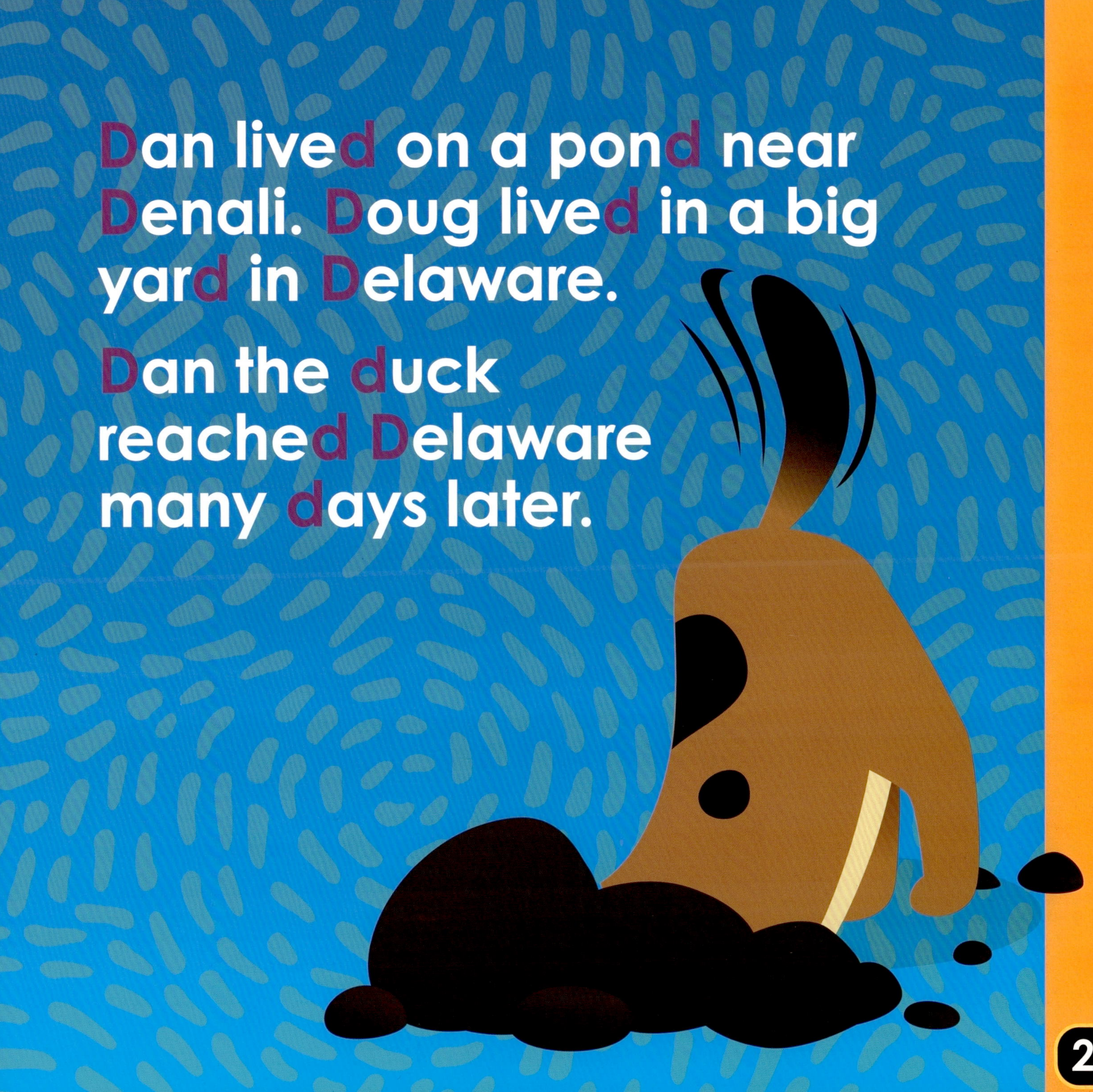

The alphabet has **26** letters.

D is the fourth letter in the alphabet.

Aa Bb Cc Dd Ee

Ff Gg Hh Ii Jj Kk

Ll Mm Nn Oo Pp

Qq Rr Ss Tt Uu Vv

Ww Xx Yy Zz

KEY WORDS

Research has shown that as much as 65 percent of all written material published in English is made up of 300 words. These 300 words cannot be taught using pictures or learned by sounding them out. They must be recognized by sight. This book contains 47 common sight words to help young readers improve their reading fluency and comprehension. This book also teaches young readers several important content words, such as proper nouns. These words are paired with pictures to aid in learning and improve understanding.

Page	Sight Words First Appearance
4	let, letter, the
5	a, an, how, is, it, this, write, you
6	can, many, start, words
8	be
10	at, end, of
12	names, water, with
13	good, likes, makes
14	different, sounds
15	in
16	food, most
17	around, day, need
18	sometimes
20	asked, he, help, him, his, often, one, to
21	big, later, near, on
22	has

Page	Content Words First Appearance
4	Dd
6	dime, dinosaur
7	dog, dolphin, duck
8	panda
9	badge, goldfish, lemonade, spider
10	red, sand
11	bird, bread, salad
12	Donna
13	Darwin, David, Deb, Dorothy, hot chocolate, pizza, presents
14	bridge, doll
18	fudge
19	badger, edge, judge, wedge
20	Dan, dirt, Doug, fun, holes
21	Delaware, Denali, pond, yard
22	alphabet

Published by Smartbook Media Inc.
276 5th Avenue, Suite 704 #917
New York, NY 10001
Website: www.openlightbox.com

Library of Congress Cataloging-in-Publication Data

Names: Rylands, Warren, author. | Siemens, Jared, author.
Title: Dd / Warren Rylands and Jared Siemens.
Description: New York, NY : Smartbook Media Inc., [2022] | Series: Learn the ABCs | Audience: Grades K-1.
Identifiers: LCCN 2020054164 (print) | LCCN 2020054165 (ebook) | ISBN 9781510557444 (library binding) | ISBN 9781510557468 (ebook other)
Subjects: LCSH: English language--Consonants--Juvenile literature. | English language--Alphabet--Juvenile literature.
Classification: LCC PE1165 .R9524 2022 (print) | LCC PE1165 (ebook) | DDC 421/.1--dc23
LC record available at https://lccn.loc.gov/2020054164
LC ebook record available at https://lccn.loc.gov/2020054165

Printed in Guangzhou, China
1 2 3 4 5 6 7 8 9 0 25 24 23 22 21

022021
110820

Art Director: Terry Paulhus **Project Coordinator:** Sara Cucini

Every reasonable effort has been made to trace ownership and to obtain permission to reprint copyright material. The publisher would be pleased to have any errors or omissions brought to its attention so that they may be corrected in subsequent printings.

The publisher acknowledges Getty Images as the primary image supplier for this title.